An Instant Guide to
AQUARIUM
FISH

*A full-color guide to identifying,
choosing and keeping aquarium fish*

ELEANOR LAWRENCE AND SUE HARNIESS

GRAMERCY BOOKS
NEW YORK

This 2001 edition is published by Gramercy Books™,
an imprint of Random House Value Publishing, Inc.,
280 Park Avenue, New York, New York 10017.

Gramercy Books™ and design are trademarks of
Random House Value Publishing, Inc.

Random House
New York • Toronto • London • Sydney • Auckland
http://www.randomhouse.com/

Printed and bound in Singapore

Library of Congress Cataloging-in-Publication Data

Lawrence, Eleanor (Eleanor C.)
    An instant guide to aquarium fish : a full-color guide to identifying, choosing, and
keeping aquarium fish / Eleanor Lawrence and Sue Harniess.
        p. cm.
    Originally published: England : Malcolm Saunders, 1991.
    ISBN 0-517-69112-4
1.   Aquarium fishes. 2. Aquariums. I. Harniess, Sue. II. Title.

    SF457 .L35 2001
    639.34—dc21

                                                                2001018992

10 9 8 7 6 5 4

Contents

Introduction

This is a brief guide to some of the most commonly available and easily kept aquarium fishes. A home aquarium is a continual source of fascination as one gets to know the habits and behavior of the individual fishes. The variety of fishes now available from dealers can be confusing and one of the main aims of this book is to provide a quick and easy guide to which fish you might like to keep, taking into account the amount of space and the time you can devote to their care.

As far as practical fishkeeping is concerned, there are three main groups of fishes. Freshwater fishes are divided into those that thrive in an unheated aquarium or outdoor pond, and those that need a heated aquarium, with the extra equipment that entails. With modern equipment, however, maintaining a heated aquarium is now no more trouble than maintaining an unheated one. Most of the freshwater fishes in this book are easy to keep, compatible with many other species, undemanding to feed, and are readily available from dealers. Some will even breed without any particular extra care. They include many delightful and colorful fishes, and a pleasing display of the smaller species can be achieved in a modestly sized tank.

The vividly colored marine fishes of tropical coral reefs and lagoons form the third group. Although their attraction is undeniable, they are more difficult for the beginner to keep than the freshwater species, and far less is known about their preferences and requirements in captivity. Even the small species need a large tank, and most are choosy as to food, very few of them being willing to take the convenient dried foods. Those illustrated in this book are reported to be amongst the easier species, but none is really recommended for a complete beginner.

In this book the fish have been grouped firstly into the three groups mentioned above, the largest section being devoted to the popular tropical freshwater fishes. This section has been further divided into smaller groupings generally recognized by fishkeepers and which are chiefly based on the biological families to which the fish belong. Within each of these smaller groups species are arranged in order of size. This is mainly to help with the choice of fish for an aquarium rather than for identification, as most of the fish seen at dealers or in home aquaria will be young or not full-grown specimens.

The Aquarium

On page 125 you will find an illustration of the equipment needed for a freshwater tropical tank. Detailed instructions on setting it up are beyond the scope of this little book and you will need to consult special books or your aquarium dealer.

Most people beginning fishkeeping would like to keep several different species in a "community" tank. In the fish descriptions we have indicated suitable species. Community tanks should ideally be no smaller than 24in/60cm long by about 12in/30cm high and 12in/30cm wide. Do not mix very large fish, however peaceful, with very small fish, and do provide shy fish with plenty of hiding places. Some fish do not thrive alone and need to be kept in small groups. Others require rather specialized conditions or are aggressive and are best kept alone or as a single pair. Choose fish that live at different levels so that they are not all competing for the same space. The number of fish you can keep in a tank depends on its surface area, not volume, and the standard recommendation is 1in of fish length (excluding tail) for every square foot of surface area. The tank lengths given in each description assume that you will be keeping several species together.

A good starting combination for a mixed tank might be a group of four small tetras (e.g. Glowlight, Neon or Lemon Tetras,) and four small barbs (e.g. Cherry or Sumatra Barbs) with a loach or a few small corydoras (e.g. Bronze Corydoras) to live at the bottom.

Plants are an essential part of any aquarium, to provide shelter and hiding places and for their decorative value. Plants suitable for most conditions include *Vallisneria*, with long strap-like leaves, Java moss (*Vesicularia*), which grows attached to rocks or roots, the floating fern *Ceratopteris*, *Egeria* with leaves in whorls, and the broad-leaved *Cryptocoryne*.

Most freshwater aquarium fish will thrive on a mixture of the readily available dried or freeze-dried foods, with additions of live food such as water fleas, tiny worms, insect larvae etc. The larvae of gnats and mosquitoes are common in water butts in the summer, and fruitflies and tiny worms are easy to culture. Variety is important, even when feeding dried food only, and one of the golden rules is not to overfeed.

Apart from a few species which breed easily without any special conditions, breeding usually requires that a pair be separated into their own tank with suitable water conditions and environment. You should consult more specialist books for details on breeding conditions for each species.

How to use this book

This book is divided into three basic sections: **Coldwater fishes**, **Tropical freshwater fishes** and **Tropical marine fishes**. These sections are clearly distinguished by the different colored bands at the top of the page (see Contents page.)

Within the freshwater fishes the different main groups have each been given a symbol, and within these smaller groups, species are arranged in order of size (final adult size.)

A diagram showing the parts of the fish body used as identification features in the descriptions can be found on page 125.

COLDWATER FISHES

All these fish except the Pumpkinseed from North America and the sticklebacks are cyprinids (the large family of fishes that includes carp as well as many tropical species) from the streams of temperate Europe and Asia. They need an unheated aquarium, with good aeration, and most can be kept outdoors in ponds in moderate climates. The main problem is overheating of small tanks or ponds in hot weather.

 Cyprinids (see page 11.)

 Sunfish: the Pumpkinseed is a member of the Centrarchidae family from North America.

 Sticklebacks: members of the family Gasterosteidae from Asia and Europe.

FRESHWATER TROPICAL FISHES

These come from the tropical and subtropical lakes, ponds, and rivers of South America (especially the Amazon,) Africa, India and Southeast Asia. A few prefer slightly brackish water.

They all require temperatures between 72° and 81°F (22°–27°C,) but otherwise have a wide range of requirements as to water quality (e.g. softness or hardness) and food. Most will take a range of the usual fish foods. Some are predominantly vegetarian and will strip any soft-leaved plants of their leaves. In the absence of any particular preference for water type, slightly soft water is best although many fishes will adapt to quite hard water from the faucet. Chlorinated water should be left to stand or treated to remove the chlorine before use. In this book, *acid* indicates a pH of 6–6.5; *slightly alkaline* a pH of 7.5–8. "Saline" indicates brackish water, which can be made by replacing 10 per cent of the water in the tank with a solution of two or three teaspoonfuls of sea salt dissolved in 2¼ gallons (10 liters) of water.

Characins: the tetras and other members of the family Characidae (the true characins,) and some related families — headstanders, pencilfishes, hatchetfish, piranhas and others. The characins and their allies include some of the most popular and easily kept aquarium fish. They are small to medium-sized, most of the commonly kept species being in the range 1¾ — 4½in (4.5–11.5cm,) from South America and Africa. They have teeth, and most have a small adipose fin. Tetras and some other characins often have an elongated, rectangular anal fin. They are active, often shoaling fish, living in the upper and middle water. Body shape varies from a symmetrical slender spindle, to a deeper-bodied (*Black Tetra*) and almost disk-like shape (the *Silver* and *Disk Tetras*.) In some the throat region is well-developed giving the fish a slightly front-heavy look. The mouth is at the end of the snout, and directed slightly upwards, indicating their preference for feeding at the surface or in mid-water. They are undemanding as to food, usually peaceable, and most will take the usual range of live and dried fish foods. The characins tend to be delicately colored, silvery, translucent or iridescent, with flashes only of bright color on body and fins, and look their best in small shoals against a dark background in a well-lit tank.

Cyprinids: a large and varied family. Tropical and subtropical species suitable for the heated aquarium include the barbs, rasboras and danios. Those kept in tropical aquaria are small to medium-sized, mostly between 1–5¾in (2.5–14.5cm.) They come from Asia, Africa and North America. Many, but not all, have one or more pairs of barbels at the edges of the jaws. They lack an adipose fin between dorsal and tail fins, and are in general more solid in appearance than the small characins, some of the smaller barbs in particular having noticeably large scales. In most species, the anal fin is smaller than in the characins, and triangular rather than rectangular. They are generally active fishes.

Bottom-living fishes: catfishes, loaches and Reedfish. The aquarium catfishes come from several related families, and are so-called because of the long barbels or "whiskers" that adorn the jaws of many species. They tend to be bottom feeders, and some species are useful scavengers in a mixed tank. They do not have the normal scaly covering but either a "naked" leathery skin (e.g. *Spotted Pimelodella*) or bony plates (the corydoras.) They like

11

plenty of hiding places and dim lighting as many are nocturnal. The loaches and the Reedfish are also included here because they have similar habits, being bottom-living, nocturnal and rather shy.

 Egglaying toothcarps: panchaxes and lyretails. These belong to the cyprinodont family, and are small brilliantly colored pike-like fishes from jungle streams in South America, Africa and Asia. Many do not require high temperatures and can even be kept in an unheated aquarium.

 Livebearing fishes: mollies, guppies, swordtails, platys and their allies. These are generally small fishes from South America and the Caribbean. They like slightly hard water. The eggs are fertilized internally and develop inside the female, who gives birth to live young.

 Cichlids: These distinctive fishes, which come mostly from Africa and the Americas, range in size from the small to quite large, over 12in (30cm,) and are becoming increasingly popular. One of their attractions is that they appear to learn to recognize their owner and become quite tame. Unlike many other fishes, one or both parents tend the eggs and young with great care. In some species the female takes the eggs into her mouth to incubate them, and young fry take cover in her mouth when alarmed.

 Anabantids or Labyrinth fishes: gouramies and fighting fish. These fish possess an extra respiratory organ as well as the gills, with which they can take in and use atmospheric air. The gouramies have pelvic fins modified as feelers. Labyrinth fishes build a "bubblenest" of air and saliva bubbles mixed with algae and pieces of plants.

 Rainbowfish: members of the family Atherinidae, characterized by the two dorsal fins.

MARINE TROPICAL FISH

The marine species kept in aquaria come from the coral reefs and shores of the Pacific and Indian Oceans and the Caribbean. The fishes in this book come from a variety of families. They require a temperature of 79°–81°F (26°–27°C) and a substrate of coarse sand or coral sand. Ready-made mixtures of salts that give "sea-water" conditions can be bought from aquarium dealers, as can the right types of rocks and corals to create a marine environment. It is best always to buy young fish as they acclimatize to captivity better and will learn to take new types of food more readily.

Specimen page

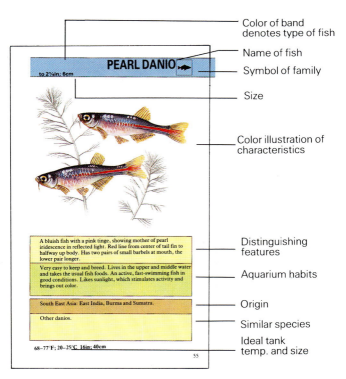

Color of band denotes type of fish

PEARL DANIO

Name of fish

Symbol of family

to 2¼in; 6cm

Size

Color illustration of characteristics

A bluish fish with a pink tinge, showing mother of pearl iridescence in reflected light. Red line from center of tail fin to halfway up body. Has two pairs of small barbels at mouth, the lower pair longer.

Distinguishing features

Very easy to keep and breed. Lives in the upper and middle water and takes the usual fish foods. An active, fast-swimming fish in good conditions. Likes sunlight, which stimulates activity and brings out color.

Aquarium habits

South East Asia: East India, Burma and Sumatra.

Origin

Other danios.

Similar species

68–77°F; 20–25°C. 16in; 40cm

Ideal tank temp. and size

55

13

An elegant, colorful small fish, with a golden line bordered with black along the side of the body and black band at base of tail. Fins tinged with bright red.

Very easy to keep and suitable for a small unheated indoor tank, although it can also be kept in a heated tank at around 72–75°F; 22–24°C. Lives in the upper water and eats the usual fish foods. Looks best when kept in a small shoal against a dark background. Breeds readily at around 72°F; 22°C.

The White Cloud Mountain near Canton in China.

Small tetras.

61–86°F; 16–30°C (but best at 64–75°F; 18–24°C) 16in; 40cm

Dull greenish brown on back with cream underside, black blotches along sides. Red patches develop around mouth and gills in the breeding season.

A coldwater fish which likes relatively shallow 6in; 15cm water. Eats insects, crustaceans and worms and will take dried food. Fairly easy to breed. Spawns April to July; the female lays her eggs on stones on the bottom.

Europe and northern Asia, in clear, cool, running water on gravel or sand.

None.

40–68°F; 4–20°C 24in; 60cm

A silvery fish with three sharp spines on back in front of the dorsal fin, which is set far back. Fan-shaped tail. In the breeding season the belly of the male becomes bright red.

Suitable for a coldwater aquarium in a small shoal but not with other species as it is carnivorous. The male becomes territorial and aggressive in the breeding season. He builds a nest of plant material to which he entices the female. He guards the eggs, and the young for a few days after hatching.

North America, Europe and northern Asia.

There are various other sticklebacks with different numbers of spines.

40–68°F; 4–20°C 24in; 60cm

to 8in; 20cm

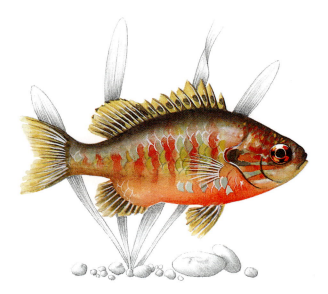

A commonly kept member of the sunfish family. The head bears many red and reddish-yellow spots and blotches. Body silvery green with reddish belly and fine reddish cross bands on back and sides.

May be kept as a pond fish or in a large well-planted tank with plenty of swimming space. It is carnivorous and needs live food, and should not be kept with other species. Likes a soft substrate. The female lays her eggs in a pit dug by the male who then guards them.

Northern USA south to Florida.

None.

46–72°F; 8–22°C 24in; 60cm

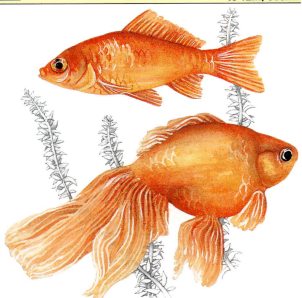

Goldfish come in several forms apart from the familiar golden-orange fish. **Veiltails** (**1**) are almost spherical with delicate, elongated fins; Comets are slim with pointed fins; Shubunkins are silver-gray/orange with black speckles.

Goldfish need a pond or unheated aquarium where the water does not become too warm. Easy to keep and long-lived in good conditions. Most types of food taken. They breed fairly readily; eggs are laid on leaf surfaces and hatch in 7 days. Veiltails should be kept in aquaria as fins are easily torn.

Originally from China but now widely found.

Orfe. The particolored black, silver and golden Koi Carp from Japan have a barbel at the side of the mouth and a more streamlined shape. They make attractive pond fish.

40–75°F; 4–24°C 20in; 50cm

A handsome streamlined fish with a silvery body and mauve-tinted fins. The Golden Orfe (illustrated) is the golden form.

Suitable for the coldwater aquarium when small but better as a pond fish. Eats snails, crustaceans and small fish, and also takes dried food. Normally breeds from April to July, the female laying many thousands of eggs on stones on the bottom.

Lakes and rivers in Europe and northern Asia.

Goldfish.

40–68°F; 4–20°C at least 24in; 60cm

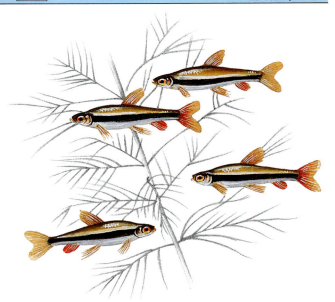

An elongated fish, golden brown above, silver below, with a lateral black stripe. Anal fin bright red, tail fin in male bright red at base. Probably a form of the duller Golden Pencilfish which grows to 3½in; 9cm.

An active peaceful fish, suitable for a small mixed tank especially with other pencilfishes. Swims in the upper and middle water. Takes small live and dried animal food and likes a dark background. Can be bred in captivity but the female lays only a few eggs at each mating.

Amazon.

One-lined Pencilfish swims head upwards; Three-lined Pencilfish: two extra brown bands bordering a gold stripe; Dwarf Pencilfish: broad dark stripes from nose to tail.

72–77°F; 22–25°C 16in; 40cm

PRISTELLA (X-RAY FISH)

to 1½in; 4cm

Body greenish above with a transparent belly through which the internal organs can be seen, giving this fish its popular name. The dorsal and anal fins bear a black blotch, the tail fin is a delicate reddish pink.

Quite easy to keep but likes a proportion of live food (e.g. small crustaceans, insects and worms) in the diet. Active and peaceful, swimming in the upper and middle water. Likes plenty of swimming space. Quite easy to breed in soft, slightly acid water and subdued light.

Northern South America.

Small tetras.

75–79°F; 24–26°C 16in; 40cm

BLACK PHANTOM TETRA

to 1¾in; 4.5cm

1

The female fish displays more color than the male, which is silvery gray with large fine fins. The **Red Phantom Tetra** (**1**) is similar, but both sexes are pink with a long, black-blotched dorsal fin.

Quite easy to keep, these small fish do best in a shoal in soft, acid water. They swim mostly near the bottom of the tank and take live and dried food. The Black Phantom is relatively easy to breed but the Red Phantom is difficult.

The Mato Grosso region of Brazil.

Some other small tetras.

73–81°F; 23–27°C 16in; 40cm

SERPAE TETRA

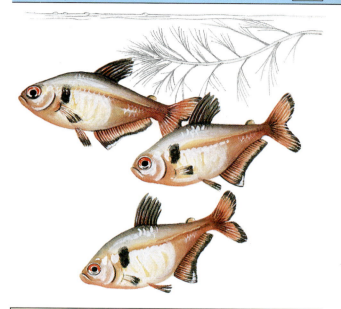

Sometimes also known as the Rosy Tetra (but see below.) A silvery fish turning to pinky red near tail. Fins, except dorsal fin, deep red. Dorsal fin mainly black and black blotch behind head. Male smaller and brighter than female.

A slow-moving and peaceable fish, easy to keep and suitable for a mixed tank. Requires soft water, a dark colored substrate to enhance coloration and takes live and dried food. Breeds fairly readily.

The Mato Grosso region of the River Paraguay.

Other tetras, especially the **Flame Tetra**. The Black Flag Tetra is also known as the Rosy Tetra. It is rosy pink with a black dorsal fin striped with white lines.

73–79°F; 23–26°C 16in; 40cm

BLACK NEON TETRA

to 1½in; 4cm

Small transparent fish with deep black stripe along side bordered
on upper edge by an iridescent line that glows in suitable lighting
conditions.

A peaceful and sociable fish, suitable for a mixed tank. Best kept
in a small shoal in a tank with a dark substrate and not too bright
lighting. Takes the usual live and dried food. Does not breed
easily.

Amazon region.

The Flag Tetra is rather similar, with a shimmering green body
and a black, red and yellow iridescent lateral stripe.

75–81°F; 24–27°C 16in; 40cm

NEON TETRA

to 1½in; 4cm

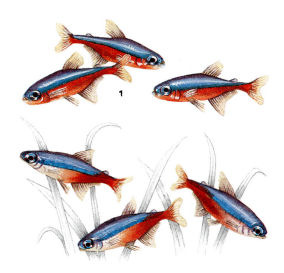

One of the most popular fish for the small aquarium, with its glowing blue-green lateral stripe. The **Cardinal Tetra** (**1**) is similar but the broad red band below the iridescent stripe extends right up to the head.

Both are active and peaceful fish, best kept in small shoals, and mix well with other species. The Neon Tetra in particular is very easy to keep, but not so easy to breed. It tends to stay near the bottom while the Cardinal Tetra prefers the middle water.

Neon Tetra: Upper Amazon. Cardinal Tetra: Upper River Negro.

None.

68–79°F; 20–26°C; (**1**) 73–79°F; 23–26°C 16in; 40cm

GLOWLIGHT TETRA

to 2in; 5cm

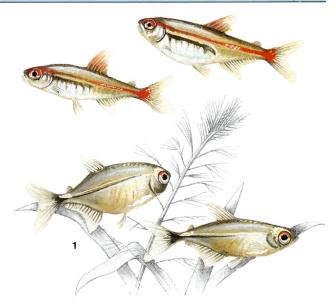

1

This almost transparent fish gains its name from the iridescent red stripe along side to base of tail and the red "glowlight" at tail base. The **Beacon Fish** (**1**) has shining yellow glowlights in the eye and base of tail.

Both are hardy and easy to keep, but dislike hard water. Best kept in small groups. Against a dark background and in dim light the iridescent markings glow as if the fish were lit from within. They like some live food in the diet. They both breed fairly easily and the Beacon Fish is very productive.

Amazon regions.

The Green Neon Tetra is similar but with a golden iridescent stripe along side and black blotch at base of tail.

73–79°F; 23–26°C 16in; 40cm

to 1½in; 4cm

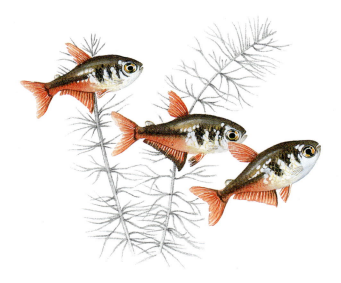

The silvery head and belly change to deep red at tail end of body. Fins, except pectorals, are blood red. Three vertical black markings at shoulder and an indistinct black line along body. Ventral and anal fins of male are edged with black.

Active and can be rather aggressive, but generally suitable for a mixed tank. Likes a well-planted tank with places to shelter and best kept in dim light to enhance color. It swims in the mid and lower water. Breeds easily, the young fry hanging from plants for the first few days.

The Rio de Janeiro area of Brazil.

Serpae Tetra and some other small tetras (e.g. Black Flag Tetra.)

68–86°F; 20–30°C 16in; 40cm

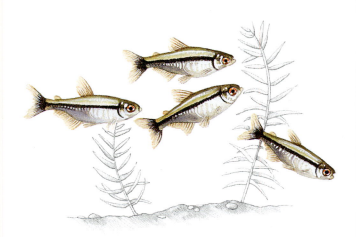

Greenish on back, silver below, with a black line along side ending in a diffuse black blotch at base of tail. Fins tinged pink.

Active and peaceable, best kept as a small shoal in a fairly large tank. Suitable for a mixed tank. Likes plant shelter but also plenty of swimming space. Easy to keep and one of the easiest tetras to breed. General conditions as for other small tetras.

Amazonia (the Para region of Brazil.)

Other rather similar tetras are the **Black Neon Tetra** and the Flag Tetra which have an iridescent line alongside the black stripe and no pink on fins.

68–73°F; 20–23°C 24in; 60cm

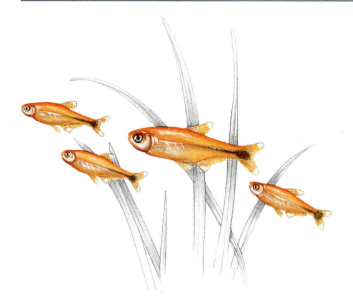

Against a dark background and lit from above, this rather colorless fish shows the distinctive and beautiful silver-tipped fins. It also has a black blotch in center of tail fin extending as a diffuse line some way up the body.

Quite easy to keep, active and sociable, and breeds readily in captivity. Should not be kept with breeding fishes as it eats spawn. Food and general conditions as for other small tetras.

Eastern Brazil.

Other small tetras. The Red-nose Tetra and the False Rummy-nose have three black and white stripes on tail and bright red on head.

68–77°F; 20–25°C 16in; 40cm

GARNET OR PRETTY TETRA

to 2in; 5cm

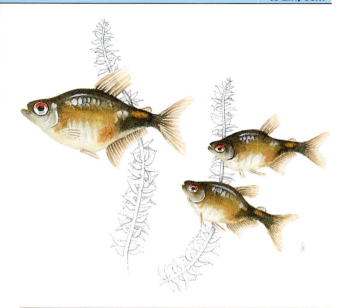

Deeper-bodied than other small tetras. Black blotch on the tail end of body. Golden line along side. Fins transparent and red-tinged. Iridescent coppery spot in front of tail fin.

Peaceful and sociable, but not particularly active. Suitable for a small mixed tank and looks best against a dark background. Likes soft, slightly acid water and a well planted shady tank. Lives in the middle water. Can be difficult to breed.

River Amazon and northern South America.

None.

73–79°F; 23–26°C 16in; 40cm

30

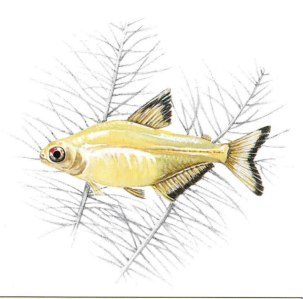

Delicate translucent yellow color on body, with more brilliant yellow on anal and dorsal fins, which also have a black edge in male. Red flash on upper half of eye.

A peaceful and active fish which may be kept with other species. Quite easy to keep but reported to be difficult to breed. General conditions as for other small tetras.

Amazonia (the Para region in Brazil.)

None.

72–75°F; 22–24°C 16in; 40cm

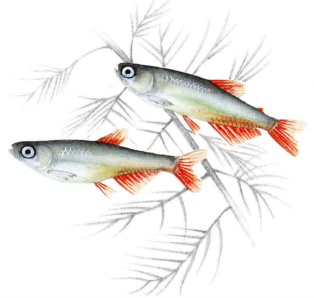

A silvery fish with fins, except pectoral, colored deep red at base becoming lighter towards margins. Pectoral fins clear. Male is slimmer with more brilliant coloring than female during the breeding season.

Active and easy to keep, taking the usual fish foods and doing best in a small shoal. Can be kept with other fish. Likes clumps of plants but also plenty of swimming space. It is relatively easy to breed, spawning at the surface, but parents must then be removed as they eat the eggs.

La Plata Basin in Amazonia.

Other similarly shaped silvery fish with red fins include the **Buenos Aires Tetra**, the **Pink-tailed Chalceus** (larger), the **Orange-finned Loach** (larger).

64–73°F; 18–23°C 16in; 40cm

to 2½in; 6.5cm

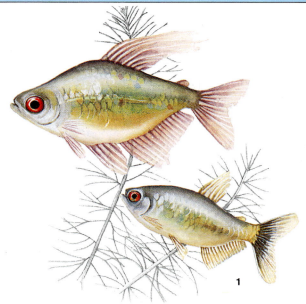

1

A silvery iridescent fish, with large fine fins, especially the elongated dorsal fin. Bright red iris to eye. The **Red-eye Tetra** (**1**) has less impressive fins and a black patch at the base of tail.

Hardy and quite easy to keep and breed. A very active swimmer, looking best in a small group. It mixes well with other fish. Likes clumps of plants to provide cover and plenty of swimming space. Takes live and dried animal food. The Red-eye Tetra is less active.

Diamond Tetra: Lake Valencia in Venezuela; Red-eye Tetra: the River Paraguay.

Other tetras.

72–79°F; 22–26°C 24in; 60cm

BLACK TETRA

to 2½in; 6.5cm

Greenish silvery ground color with two dark vertical bars at front
end of body; black-tinged towards tail. Large curved anal fin. The
black fades to gray as the fish gets larger. There is a veiltail form.

Attractive when small and kept in a small shoal, which moves in
strict formation. Very easy to keep and good for the community
tank. Likes some clumps of plants for shelter. Eats live and dried
animal food. Easy to breed.

River Negro and River Paraguay in South America.

The smaller Griem's Tetra (1¼in; 3cm) has vertical black bars but
a bright red tail end.

73–77°F; 23–25°C 16in; 40cm

34

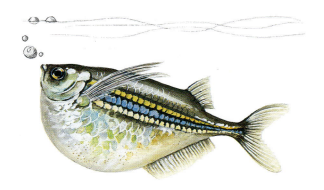

Silvery grayish yellow fish with a laterally flattened body of distinctive shape. Thin black, blue and yellow lines lead from back of head to base of tail. Elongated pectoral fins.

A surface-living fish which, in its natural habitat, can glide several meters over the surface of the water, so tank needs a close-fitting lid. Can be kept with other fish, especially those that live in the middle and lower waters. Takes live and dried food. Very rarely breeds in captivity.

Middle and lower Amazon and other parts of central and northern South America.

The Silver Hatchetfish is very similar but more delicate. Several other hatchetfish are now also kept in aquaria.

75–79°F; 24–26°C 24in; 60cm

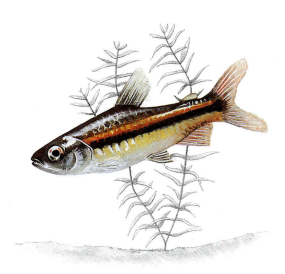

Reddish brown back shades to a whitish belly. A dark horizontal line on side, bordered with yellow, runs from head to tail. Anal and tail fins tinged pink or red.

Hardy and peaceful, suitable for a mixed tank with a sandy bottom. No special requirements but likes live food and breeds readily in captivity, laying its eggs among fine-leaved plants.

Equatorial West Africa from the Congo to the Nile.

Despite its name this fish belongs to a different family from the other tetras and characins.

75–79°F; 24–26°C 24in; 60cm

BOEHLKE'S PENGUIN FISH

to 3in; 7.5cm

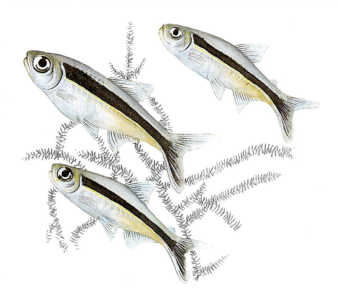

A silvery green fish with a distinctive thick black stripe along the side from gills to end of lower lobe of tail fin. Below this is an iridescent gold line. Belly pinkish. It adopts a typical oblique resting position with head upwards.

Relatively easy to keep but rather shy, doing best in a small group. Although it rests at an oblique angle it swims horizontally. Likes plenty of plant cover and floating plants to provide shade. Takes live and dried food. Can jump out of the tank if not kept securely covered.

Amazon Basin.

Penguin Fish: black stripe only starts behind the dorsal fin. The One-lined Pencilfish has a similar stripe, but is much slimmer. It also swims in the oblique position.

73–81°F; 23–27°C 24in; 60cm

37

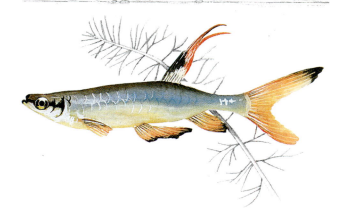

Elongated, slender fish with a greeny blue body shading to a yellow belly. Black line through eye. Fins yellow with reddish tips. In the male the fins are black-tipped and the dorsal and upper tail fins are elongated and pointed.

A surface-living fish, best kept in a shoal. It gets its name from the curious reproductive behavior. The female lays her eggs on a leaf or stem out of the water, and to prevent them drying up the male continually splashes them with his tail. Quite easy to keep and breed. Likes some dense vegetation.

The lower Amazon.

The Fanning Characin is similar in shape but lacks the black stripe through eye and has more rounded tail and dorsal fins.

72–81°F; 22–27°C 16in; 40cm

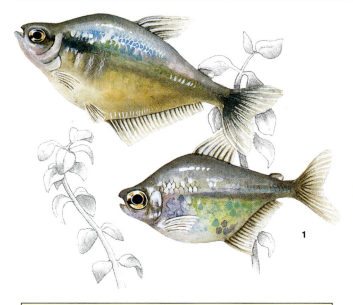

Bluish silver, with a somewhat diamond shaped body, laterally compressed. Blue-black blotch on shoulder.

Hardy and easy to keep. Generally peaceable and active and can be kept with other species of same size, but may nibble the fins of other fish. Best kept as a shoal. It may eat the leaves of soft plants in the aquarium.

Fresh water near coasts of Guyana and Venezuela.

The **Disk Tetra** (1) is the same shape with iridescent flanks and dark-bordered scales, but no ventral fin or black blotch.

68–73°F; 20–23°C 20in; 50cm

BUENOS AIRES TETRA

to 4¼in; 11cm

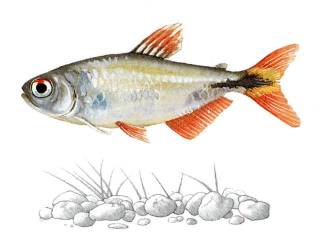

A silvery fish, tinged greenish above. One of the larger tetras. Carries a black diamond-shaped mark at base of tail. Fins of male are red, dorsal fin with a red blotch. Fins of female are almost colorless.

Hardy and easy to keep, but can be aggressive to other fish, biting their fins. Like most tetras requires soft water. Greedy, and will take all sorts of food. Relatively easy to breed.

River de la Plata in South America.

Other fishes with a silvery body and reddish fins include the **Bloodfin** (smaller,) the **Pink-tailed Chalceus** and the **Orange-finned Loach.**

64–77°F; 18–25°C 24in; 60cm

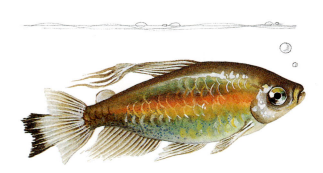

One of the larger tetras, a colorless fish with an elongated dorsal fin, only showing its brilliant iridescence when lit from above or from the front. Only males have the characteristic feathery tail fin.

An active fish, best kept in a small shoal. Mixes well with other larger tetras but needs plenty of swimming space. Prefers to feed at surface, taking live and dried food. Productive and fairly easy to breed.

The basin of the River Congo in Africa.

The Long-finned African Tetra has a black blotch at base of tail.

73–79°F; 23–26°C 24in; 60cm

A silvery fish with slightly elongated snout and regular dark spots on body and dorsal fin. It adopts a typical head down feeding position.

An active fish which likes a well-planted tank with dense clumps of tall plants and a dark background. Can be kept with other species. Takes live food such as small insect larvae from bottom, plant fragments and dried food. Not easy to breed.

Northeastern South America.

Other headstanders are the black and white Striped Headstander and the more bulky blackish Headstander.

70–81°F; 21–27°C 16–20in; 40–50cm

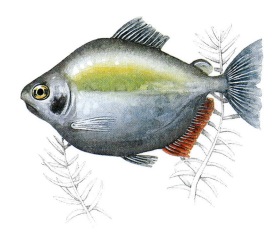

Body much flattened sideways to resemble a thin silver disk, which gives this fish its popular name of Dollarfish. Red-tinged anal fin. Young fish have various dark markings, which disappear with age.

Relatively easy to keep and undemanding as to food. A rather shy, shoaling fish, suitable for a large community tank. It is, however, herbivorous, and will eat any soft-leaved plants in the tank. Provide rocks and roots for hiding places.

Amazon Basin.

The Silver Pacu or Dollar is also disk-like with a red anal fin, but is not herbivorous. It has a black spot on gill cover.

75–81°F; 24–27°C 24in; 60cm

PINK-TAILED CHALCEUS

to 10in; 25cm

Long slender fish with bluish silvery body, large scales and pink fins.

An active, surface-living fish with a tendency to jump out of the water. Best kept in a small shoal in a large well-lit tank with a close-fitting lid. Can be kept with other species. Eats animal food and likes earthworms.

The Guyanas.

The Rainbow Shark (3in; 7.5cm) has a large dorsal fin and a black blotch at base of tail.

73–81°F; 23–27°C 24in; 60cm

A high-backed fish with six black cross bands on a golden ground. All fins, except pectorals, are red.

Shy and peaceable, and suitable for the home aquarium when small. Likes to hide, and will eat soft-leaved plants. Likes plenty of vegetable material in diet (e.g. spinach, lettuce,) and also takes other usual fish foods.

The lower and middle Congo River in Africa.

Banded Loach (much smaller.)

75–81°F; 24–27°C 24in; 60cm

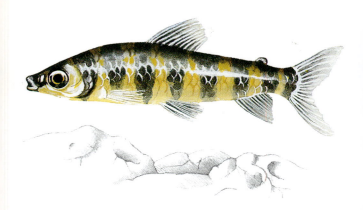

Upper lip cleft, as in other Leporinus species. Adults generally have nine black bands on a yellow ground; younger fish have fewer.

A generally peaceable and sluggish fish, which eventually may grow too large for the home aquarium. Often swims head down in the lower water. Likes plenty of vegetable material in the diet (e.g. lettuce and oatflakes.) Can jump out of the water, so the tank needs a close-fitting lid.

South America.

The Striped Leporinus with several dark horizontal stripes on body, has similar habits and requires similar conditions.

70–79°F; 21–26°C 20in; 50cm (for smaller fish.)

to 14in; 35cm

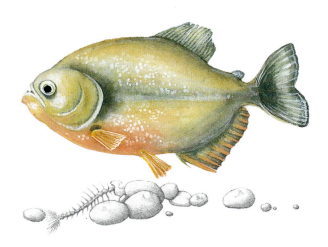

A deep-bodied fish, silvery and disk-like when small. Very sharp powerful teeth. Underside and anal fin becoming reddish in bigger fish. Tail fin has distinct dark border.

Attractive in shoals when small, but cannot be kept with other fish as it is aggressive and carnivorous. It should be handled with extreme care. Larger fish are not suitable for the home aquarium. Eats raw meat, fish, insects, etc.

Amazon and Orinoco basins.

There are several species of piranha, the White or Spotted Piranha being the most aggressive.

75–81°F; 24–27°C 36in; 90cm

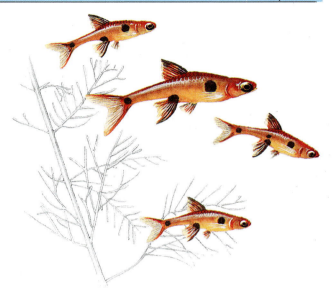

The body is reddish shading to an orange belly, with a large dark spot just behind the gill cover and another smaller one at the base of the tail. One dot at the base of the anal fin denotes a male, two a female. Fins reddish.

This tiny fish looks its best in a shoal against a dark background and illuminated from the front. An active fish, suitable for a mixed tank with other small species. Likes a densely planted tank with some broad-leaved plants to give shade. Difficult to breed.

Malaysia.

None.

70–77°F; 21–25°C 16in; 40cm

to 1¾in; 4.5cm

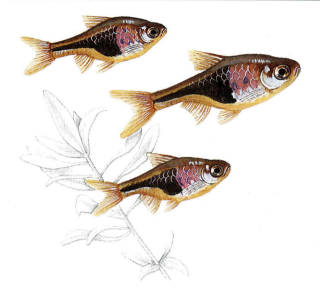

Often also known simply as "Rasbora," this small fish has a wedge-shaped black mark covering most of the tail end of body, extending forwards to the ventral fin. The male is more slender with the black marking extending right down to belly.

A peaceful, shoaling fish, good for a mixed tank, especially with other small rather delicate fish, or very effective as a shoal on its own. Likes soft water and a peat substrate. Not difficult to keep but quite difficult to breed. The eggs are laid on the underside of broad-leaved plants.

Thailand, Malaysia and Sumatra.

None.

75–81°F; 24–27°C 16in; 40cm

1

A small streamlined fish with thin silver horizontal stripes on a blue-black background. Tail and anal fins also striped. In the less popular **Leopard Danio** (**1**) the stripes break up into spots towards the tail.

One of the easiest fish to keep. Very hardy with no special requirements. Active, swimming near the surface. Good in a mixed tank with other fast-swimming fish. Likes plenty of swimming space. Easy to breed.

Zebra Danio: India. Leopard Danio: Burma.

None.

72–77°F; 22–25°C 16in; 40cm

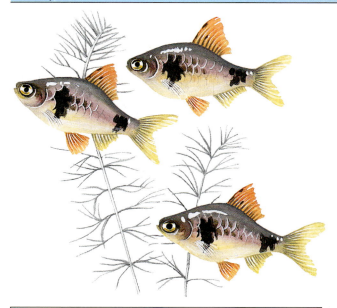

A small deep-bodied fish, with a silvery body, darker on back, and two dark vertical bars behind head and near tail. Fins variable in color from red to yellow. No barbels.

Easy to keep in conditions similar to other small barbs. Best kept as a small shoal, which tends to swim in the middle and lower water. Takes the usual fish foods. Can be bred in captivity but, like the other barbs, parents must be removed after spawning as they tend to eat the eggs.

Mountain streams in Sri Lanka.

See other barbs.

75–81°F; 24–27°C 16in; 40cm

Body silver, darker on back, with a black horizontal line along side bordered above with a band of gold from nose to base of tail. Fins red. One pair of barbels at mouth. In the breeding season the male becomes pink or red.

Active, peaceful but rather shy and keeps its distance from other species. Likes dim lighting and plenty of plant cover, including floating plants for shade. Takes live and dried food. Not very easy to breed.

Sri Lanka.

Half-banded Barb; Black Ruby Barb; Rosy Barb.

73–79°F; 23–26°C 16in; 40cm

CHECKER BARB

to 2in; 5cm

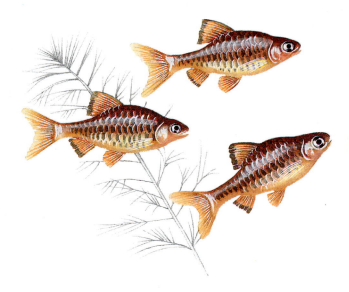

A handsome small fish with large reflective scales, each with a black base, giving it a checkerboard appearance. The ground color is a light reddish brown. Fins are tinged with orange, more intense in the male. Pair of small barbels at mouth.

A peaceful and sociable fish. Likes a peat substrate to bottom of tank. General conditions as for other small barbs. Suitable for a mixed tank. Breeds fairly readily, the eggs sticking to plants after spawning.

Sumatra.

None.

73–75°F; 23–24°C 16in; 40cm

53

BLACK RUBY BARB

to 2¼in; 6cm

Out of the breeding season both male and female are greenish gray with darker vertical bands. In season the male becomes a deep ruby red on head and front end of body, especially when excited.

An active and sociable fish, very easy to keep, taking the usual fish foods. Likes a tank with dark substrate and roots for hiding places, as well as some bright places, but becomes colorless in very bright light. Breeds readily especially if fed some live food.

Shady mountain streams in Sri Lanka.

Rosy Barb; Cherry Barb.

66–77°F; 19–25°C 16in; 40cm

54

PEARL DANIO

to 2¼in; 6cm

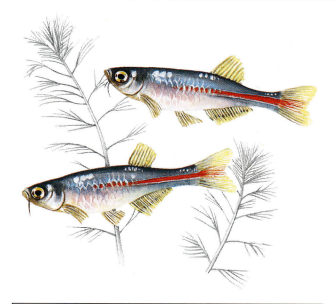

A bluish fish with a pink tinge, showing mother of pearl iridescence in reflected light. Red line from center of tail fin to halfway up body. Has two pairs of small barbels at mouth, the lower pair longer.

Very easy to keep and breed. Lives in the upper and middle water and takes the usual fish foods. An active, fast-swimming fish in good conditions. Likes sunlight, which stimulates activity and highlights beauty.

South East Asia: East India, Burma and Sumatra.

Other danios.

68–77°F; 20–25°C 16in; 40cm

GOLDEN BARB

to 2¾in; 7cm

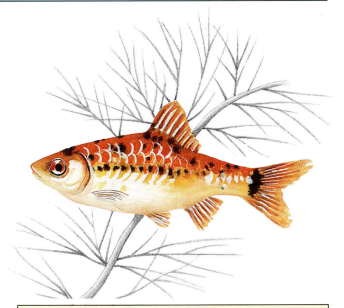

Clear golden yellow on body with orange-brown fins. Sparse irregular dark spots and blotches on body. No barbels.

Very easy to keep and breed, with no special requirements. Good for a mixed tank where it swims in the upper and middle water. Likes clumps of plants to hide in. Breeds in shallow water, laying the eggs in dense vegetation.

Thought to be a form of the Half-banded Barb.

The **Lemon Tetra** is paler, smaller-scaled and with a wide anal fin.

68–75°F; 20–24°C 16in; 40cm

A rather drab light greenish brown in color with several vertical blotches on side and a yellow tinge to the fins. In the breeding season the male becomes brighter and takes on a reddish tinge. The back becomes higher in older individuals.

Hardy, easy to keep and easy to breed. Lives in the middle and bottom water and digs in the substrate. Likes clear, well aerated water and clumps of plants to hide in. Before spawning, the male circles the female, touching her with nose and tail, and trying to push her into the vegetation.

Southeastern China.

Other small barbs have a similar shape. The **Golden Barb** is thought to be a form of this species.

63–77°F; 17–25°C 16in; 40cm

Several species and subspecies are known as Tiger Barbs. *B. tetrazona* is one of the most striking and easy to keep. It has four dark cross bands and bright red fins.

An active and somewhat aggressive fish, living in the middle water, sometimes not considered suitable for a mixed tank. Best kept in a shoal. Takes the usual fish foods and breeds easily, producing up to 1000 eggs at a time.

Sumatra and Borneo.

Other Tiger Barbs are *B. pentazona* with five bands and *B. hexazona* with six bands. *B. t. partipentazona* has a half band extending down from dorsal fin. All have red or reddish fins.

68–77°F; 20–25°C 24in; 60cm

TIC-TAC-TOE BARB

to 2¾in; 7cm

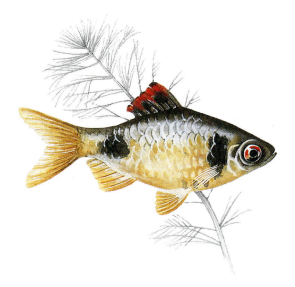

Silvery fish with a yellow tinge and marked with two blurred spots, one behind the gill cover, the other above the anal fin. Fins translucent and yellow tinged. The dorsal fin is bordered with red in the male.

Very active but peaceable fish, good for a mixed tank. Best kept as a shoal. Likes bright light but also some dense clumps of vegetation. Easy to keep and breeds fairly readily, spawning among the plants. Takes the usual fish foods, including some vegetable matter.

India and Sri Lanka.

Stoliczka's Barb is very similar but stouter and the dorsal fin of male is bright red with black markings.

73–79°F; 23–26°C 24in; 60cm

GIANT DANIO

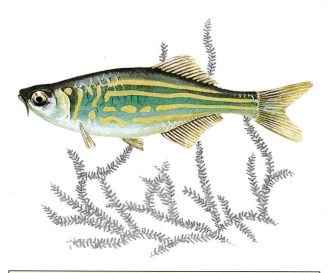

A bluish fish with several yellow lines along side from back of head to tail fin. One pair of barbels at mouth. Fins become red in the breeding season.

An active and fast-swimming fish, best kept as a shoal. Lives in the upper water and takes the usual fish foods. Easy to keep with no special requirements. A prolific breeder, spawning among fine-leaved plants and producing up to 1000 eggs at a time.

Western coasts of India and Sri Lanka.

The rather similar Bengal Danio is greenish shading to silver below, with indistinct blue-green stripes from center of body to tail fin.

75–79°F; 24–26°C 24in; 60cm

FLYING FOX

Gray back, silvery sides and belly with a broad horizontal black stripe from snout right into tail fin. Downward directed mouth with two pairs of barbels.

Territorial and can become aggressive to others of the same species, so a large tank is needed. A bottom living fish which helps keep tank glass clean as it grazes on algae. Otherwise it eats the usual fish foods. Has not yet been bred in captivity.

Borneo and Sumatra.

None.

72–77°F; 22–25°C 36in; 90cm

RED-TAILED SHARK

to 4¾in; 12cm

In reality has nothing in common with the true shark family. It is a striking fish with velvety black body and a bright contrasting red tail. It has two pairs of small barbels.

Likes subdued light and a tank with hiding places among rocks. Can be aggressive towards other members of the same species so best as a single individual in a community tank. Takes the usual fish foods and also eats algae. Rarely bred in captivity.

Thailand.

Black Shark.

77°F; 25°C 24in; 60cm

ROSY BARB

to 5½in; 14cm

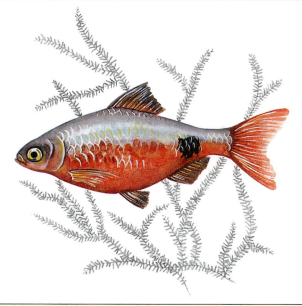

A silvery fish with a blue-green sheen. Males develop deep rosy red on sides, belly and fins in breeding season; females red on fins only. Black blotch on tail end of body. No barbels.

Very easy to keep with no special requirements. Can be kept with other fish. Breeds readily in captivity in dense vegetation. Best kept in a shoal and likes bright light.

Flowing streams and rivers in northeastern India.

Several other barbs have red fins.

68–77°F; 20–25°C 24in; 60cm

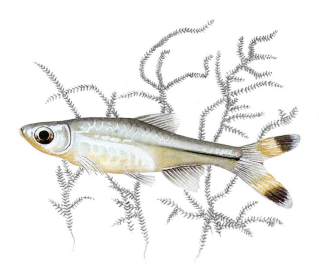

A slender fish with a silvery greenish body and distinctive tail markings, black and orange with clear tips. A black line also extends from base of tail halfway along side of body. The lobes of the tail fin open and close like scissors.

Active and fast-swimming, suitable for a mixed tank with fish the same size. Needs plenty of swimming space. Eats dried and live animal food. Not easy to breed, as it rarely gets large enough in captivity.

Southern Malaya, Singapore and Sumatra.

None.

75–79°F; 24–26°C 24in; 60cm

A deep-bodied fish with the back becoming high with age. Derives its popular name from the silver body turning to cream on the belly.

A fine fish for the home aquarium when small but grows rapidly and soon becomes too large. It is vegetarian and unless given plenty of plant food will strip the plants in the tank. It has rarely been bred in captivity.

Sumatra, Borneo, Malaysia and Thailand.

None.

68–77°F; 20–25°C 36in; 90cm

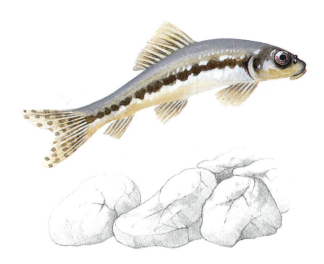

A round-bodied, elongated fish with a downward pointing mouth, the thick lips forming a rasping sucker. Body beige with dark markings along sides and spots on fins. Grows up to 12in; 30cm in the wild.

An active fish, best kept in a large, well-planted aquarium, where it is one of the best species for removing algae. It lives on the bottom or clings to the tank glass. Can be kept with other species but becomes aggressive when older. As well as algae, eats vegetable and dried foods.

Thailand.

None.

68–86°F; 20–30°C 24in; 60cm

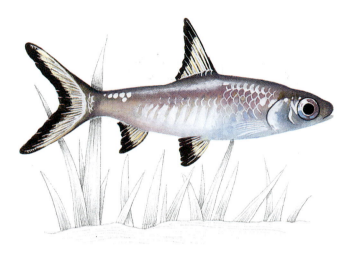

This handsome shark-shaped fish has yellow-tinged, black-edged fins that contrast with the silver body. It is in reality a member of the carp family (cyprinids.)

Attractive when kept in a small shoal when young, but will soon outgrow all but the largest home aquarium. An active fish, suitable for a large community tank with other suitably sized fishes. Eats the usual live and dried foods.

Borneo, Sumatra and Thailand.

None.

75°F; 24°C 36in; 90cm

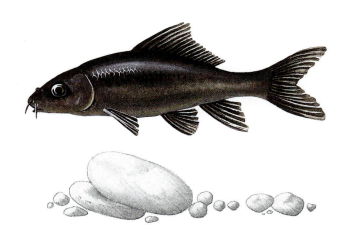

So-called from its shark-like appearance. All black, with two pairs of barbels at mouth.

A rather shy fish, despite its rather awesome appearance when large. It is only suitable for the home aquarium when small. Eats algae and scavenges on the bottom of the tank; also eats the usual fish foods. Can be kept with other fish.

Southeast Asia.

Red-tailed Shark.

72–81°F; 22–27°C 24in; 60cm or larger

68

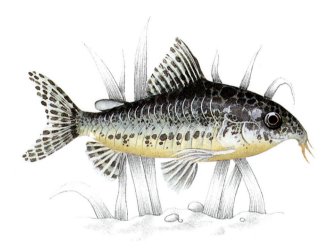

One of the armored catfishes, with two rows of smooth overlapping bony plates on sides. Dull blue-green back with pale belly, blotched and spotted with black. Fins, except pectorals and pelvics, spotted. Two pairs of barbels.

Omnivorous and a good scavenger, a useful and peaceable bottom-living member of a community tank. Very easy and undemanding to keep and breeds readily. It likes a soft substrate for burrowing, soft to slightly alkaline water and prefers subdued lighting.

Slow-flowing rivers in the La Plata Basin, in Brazil.

Aeneus Catfish. Leopard Corydoras is blue-gray with black spots; Black-spotted Corydoras and Network Catfish have pale bodies with dark markings.

64–84°F; 18–29°C 16in; 40cm

An armored catfish with two rows of bony plates along the sides. Golden yellow body with copper colored patch on head and along back. Two pairs of drooping barbels around mouth.

Like other corydoras, it is omnivorous and a good scavenger, a useful bottom-living member of a community tank. Easy to keep and relatively easy to breed. Likes a sandy substrate for burrowing.

Trinidad, northern South America: Venezuela to the River de la Plata.

See **Peppered Catfish.**

64–84°F; 18–29°C 16in; 40cm

1

Sinuous and eel-like with a golden-brown body cross banded with ten or so wide black bands. The **Clown Loach** (**1**) (up to 12in; 30cm in the wild) is thick-bodied and high-backed with three black cross bands.

Nocturnal, bottom-living fishes that burrow into the substrate and move around the bases of plants. Eat dried and vegetable food and are also fond of worms, which will tempt them out of hiding. Food should be given on the bottom. Need soft water. The Coolie Loach can be kept in a community tank.

Kuhli Loach: Malaya; Clown Loach: Borneo and Sumatra.

The Half-striped Kuhli Loach has a less distinct pattern and the dorsal fin further forward. The Banded Loach is more like the Clown Loach in shape; ground color beige with around eleven darker bands.

81°F; 27°C Kuhli Loach: 16in; 40cm; Clown Loach: 20in; 50cm

Greenish gray, slightly high-backed body, fins all pinky orange. There is a diffuse black blotch at base of tail and three pairs of barbels around the mouth.

Shy and nocturnal, becoming quite active at night. Rather intolerant of other fish and best kept as a single individual in a community tank. Like other loaches it lives on the bottom, taking dried and live food, which should be given on the bottom.

Thailand, Vietnam and Malaya.

None amongst the loaches; other fish with pink or orange fins are the **Pink-tailed Characin** and the much smaller **Bloodfin** and **Buenos Aires Tetra**.

75–84°F; 24–29°C 24in; 60cm

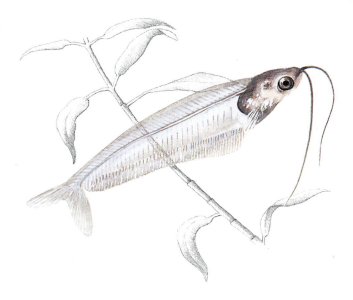

This fascinating fish is almost totally transparent, revealing the skeleton in finest detail. Internal organs are clustered in a dark area behind the head. There are two long barbels or "whiskers" on the upper jaw.

Despite its appearance this is a hardy fish and easy to keep. Best in a shoal in a well-planted tank with enough free space. It is peaceable and mixes well with other small tolerant species. Lives in the middle water, adopting an oblique, head-up position with tail constantly moving.

Southeast Asia.

None.

68–79°F; 20–26°C 24in; 60cm

An elongated, graceful fish, with a skin lacking scales or other bony covering. Pale gray ground color with spots and blotches of darker gray on body and fins. Three pairs of long barbels around mouth.

Peaceable and mainly nocturnal, scavenging on the bottom. Needs hiding places, soft water and subdued lighting. May be kept in a community tank with other suitable species, where it is useful in clearing scraps of uneaten food from the bottom. Likes live food such as insects and worms.

Central South America.

Slender Pimelodella with greeny brown body and dark line along side; Striped Catfish with horizontal stripes of white and dark blue gray.

64–75°F; 18–24°C 20in; 50cm

Gray-brown body with darker spots and patches on body and fins. Five darker cross bands on body. Sucker-like mouth on underside of head with one pair of barbels above. Beware the spine on dorsal fin when handling.

Mainly nocturnal and rather shy. Good at removing algae from tank glass and plants. Prefers medium hard, slightly brackish (saline) water. May be kept in a community tank but can be aggressive when new members are introduced. As well as algae, eats worms, dried and vegetable foods.

Southern Brazil.

The Whiptail is slimmer and elongated, with a smaller dorsal fin, and a whip-like extension to upper lobe of tail fin.

75°F; 24°C 24in; 60cm

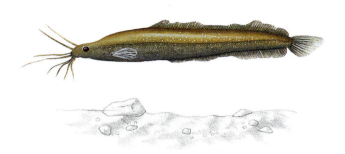

This large catfish is a "naked" catfish, having no scales or bony plates on the surface. Four pairs of barbels around the mouth. It is a dull gray-blue with a bronze sheen on the back and small white spots on side.

A greedy predatory fish, which should be kept on its own and fed on live food such as worms, insects and fresh meat. Will also take dried food. Lives on the bottom and likes a soft substrate to burrow in, and soft water. Only suitable for the home aquarium when young.

India, Ceylon and Southeast Asia.

There is also an albino form.

68–77°F; 20–25°C 40in; 100cm

A dull brownish snake-like fish. Males and females can be distinguished by the number of rays on the anal fin: males have 12–14, females 9–12.

Peaceful, rather shy and nocturnal, moving like a snake over the bottom of tank, sometimes burying itself. Eats a variety of animal food. It can breathe air and rises to the surface to breathe. It can be kept with other fish but gets too large for the average home aquarium.

Tropical Africa: the Niger delta and Cameroons.

None.

72–81°F; 22–27°C at least 36in; 90cm

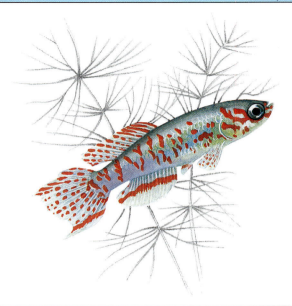

An egg-laying toothcarp, with a blue-green body lavishly speckled with red dots on body and fins. Female lacks the extended rays on tail and anal fins and is duller in color.

Best kept as a single pair in their own tank. Likes a densely planted tank with surface cover and soft substrate. Lives mainly in the middle water. Takes live and dried food. Prefers soft, acid and peaty water. Spawns on or near the bottom.

West Africa.

Lyretail.

68–75°F; 20–24°C 16in; 40cm

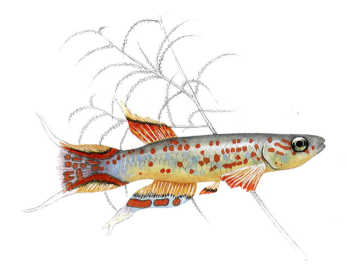

An egg-laying toothcarp. Brightly colored with silvery sides dotted with red, upper and lower borders of the lyre-shaped tail fin are orange with white tips. Red spots on tail and anal fins have dark borders. There is a golden form.

Requires soft, slightly acid water with a peat substrate. Prefers a densely planted tank with roots and rocks for hiding places. Eats live and dried foods. Breeds best in very soft water, laying eggs on fine-leaved plants. Best kept in their own aquarium.

Shady ponds in equatorial Africa: Cameroon, Gabon and Zaire.

Togo Lyretail.

73–82°F; 23–28°C 16in; 40cm

One of the egg-laying toothcarp family, like a tiny pike in shape, with the mouth on top of the snout. Body color of male very variable, usually a ground of olive brown with blue dots and orange fins. Black blotch on base of dorsal fin.

Surface-living and feeding, predatory but will tolerate fish of the same size in a community tank. One of the easiest toothcarps to keep and to breed. Eggs are laid amongst fine-leaved plants. Likes soft water, and a well planted tank with floating plants covering part of the surface.

India and Southeast Asia.

The Green Panchax is smaller, with mottled greenish body and fins; the Ceylon Panchax has a pointed anal fin and black blotches on body.

75–79°F; 24–26°C 16in; 40cm

to 2¼in; 6cm female; 1¼in; 3cm male

Many colorful and large-finned forms of this popular live-bearing fish have been bred. Fin pattern in males very variable, with red, blue, yellow and orange predominant. The wild female is larger than the male and dull in color.

Hardy and peaceable, very easy to keep and to breed. Can be kept in a community tank, preferring medium hard, alkaline, saline water. Takes the usual dried and live foods and also eats algae.

Northern South America.

None.

68–75°F; 20–24°C 16in; 40cm

PLATY

to 2¼in; 6cm female; 1¾in; 4.5cm male

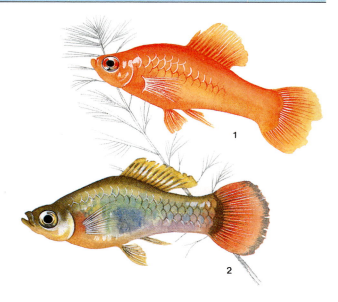

1

2

A live-bearer, the wild form has a greenish body tinged with blue. Various colored forms have been bred, including the familiar **Red Platy** (**1**.) The wild **Variatus Platy** (**2**) male is olive green speckled with various colors.

Both are hardy and easy to keep, tolerating a wide range of conditions. They prefer slightly hard and alkaline water, and like a well-planted tank and plenty of light. Easy to breed. May be kept in a community tank.

Platy: ponds and lakes in Central America; Variatus Platy: Mexico.

None.

72–81°F; 22–27°C 16in; 40cm

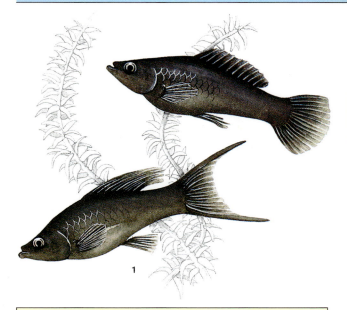

1

A live-bearing toothcarp, the fertilized eggs developing and hatching inside the female's body. Several varieties of this popular all-black fish have been bred, including a lyretail form (**1**.)

Easy to keep and to breed. Like all mollies it feeds continuously and needs a sunny tank to supply algae and plant growth, and also requires frequent feeds of live and dried food. Prefers slightly saline water.

Southwestern United States through Central America to Venezuela.

None.

73–82°F; 23–28°C 16in; 40cm

A live-bearing toothcarp, body greeny yellow with light and dark patterned scales. The large iridescent spotted dorsal fin of the male is often displayed erect. The female has much smaller dorsal and tail fins.

Best kept as a single pair, either on their own or in a community tank. Needs plenty of swimming space in a well-planted tank with rocks and roots for hiding places. Water medium hard and slightly saline. Likes plenty of green food as well as the usual dried and live foods.

Estuaries in the southeastern United States.

The Yucatan Sailfin Molly is very similar but larger.

68–75°F; 20–24°C 20in; 50cm

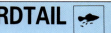
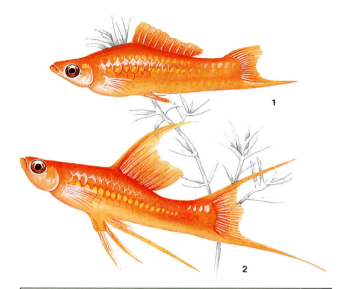

1

2

Several brightly colored forms of this live-bearing species have been bred, including orange (**1**) and lyretail (**2**) varieties. The lower lobe of tail fin is elongated to form the "sword" in the male. The wild form is greenish silver.

An active fish, easy to keep and breed, but greedy, only suitable for a community tank with larger species. Requires plenty of swimming space, and dense vegetation for hiding places. Water medium hard and slightly alkaline. Eats the usual dried and live foods.

Mexico, Guatemala, and Honduras.

Females of orange forms may resemble the red forms of the smaller **Platy** (to 2¾in; 4cm.)

68–77°F; 20–25°C 20in; 50cm

FOUR-EYES

to 8in; 20cm

A live-bearing fish, characterized by the protruding eyes on top of the head. Yellow brown body very elongated with a rounded tail fin and small dorsal fin set far back.

Generally found at surface, swimming with the upper half of the eye above the surface. Requires a large water surface area, but not deep water. Takes live insects at the surface. May be kept in a spacious community tank with plenty of plant cover and a tight-fitting lid. Water hardish, saline.

Northern and central South America.

None.

72–79°F; 22–26°C 24in; 60cm

A small cichlid, the male having a lilac body with a metallic sheen. The dorsal fin has a purple bar at base. The tail fin is bordered with white. Female smaller and less brightly colored, with a rounded tail fin.

Quite easy to keep and to breed, and may be kept with other species. Before spawning, the male cleans a spawning site and the male and female look after the young fry. Likes soft, acid and peaty water, and takes the usual live and dried food.

Amazon basin.

Other small cichlids: Reitzig's Dwarf Cichlid has a silvery body and blue tinged fins; Golden Dwarf Cichlid is a rather dull greenish brown.

73–77°F; 23–25°C 20in; 50cm

The silvery body changes color with great rapidity, varying from pale blue to purple with belly and anal fin turning deep red, and flashes of yellow and other colors appearing on body and fins.

A peaceable, omnivorous cichlid, living mainly near the bottom. May be kept with other species. Requires saline water. Eggs are guarded by both parents in typical cichlid fashion.

Coastal areas of Nigeria, West Africa.

Egyptian Mouthbrooder.

75–81°F; 24–27°C 24in; 60cm

EGYPTIAN MOUTHBROODER

to 3¼in; 8cm

A beautiful small cichlid. The back is dark purple shading
through blue and green to a pale yellowish belly. Scales are silver-
edged. Tail, anal and dorsal fins are speckled with bluish white
dots. Red edge to anal fin in male.

One of the mouthbrooding cichlids, the female keeping the eggs,
and later the young fry, in the mouth to guard them. It is a hardy
fish, with no particular requirements as to water quality, easy to
keep and quite easy to breed. Takes a varied diet including tiny
pieces of fresh meat.

The Nile from Egypt to Tanzania.

Kribensis.

75–81°F; 24–27°C 24in; 60cm

ORANGE CHROMIDE

to 3¼in; 8cm

The orange-beige ground color of this cichlid changes to a rich green on sides in the breeding season. There are horizontal rows of red dots on body and fins are marked with dark dots. Often bears a large dark spot halfway along body.

This is a rather delicate fish which requires hard and saline water. It is peaceable and may be kept with other small fishes that require similar conditions. Unlike some cichlids it does not attack the plants. Takes a varied diet.

Coastal regions of India and Sri Lanka.

The much larger Banded Chromide (to 16in; 40cm in the wild) is a dull greenish gray, becoming more brilliantly colored when breeding.

68–79°F; 20–26°C 20in; 50cm

90

One of the brightly colored mouthbrooding cichlids from Lake Malawi sometimes known as Nyasa cichlids. The male is always a bright blue, with red and orange on dorsal and anal fins. Female may be blue, or marbled duller gray, brown and orange.

Rather aggressive and should be kept in their own spacious aquarium, in medium hard water. They are vegetarian, also taking a range of live and dried foods. Like plenty of rocks for cover. The female incubates the eggs in her mouth.

Lake Malawi.

The larger Malawi Blue Cichlid is deeper bodied, lacks the orange-red dorsal fin and has around six dark vertical bars on sides.

75–81°F; 24–27°C 36in; 90cm

A laterally flattened, disk-shaped cichlid. The grayish brown body is barred with darker blue-gray, but coloring is very variable.

Peaceable, shoaling fish, best kept on their own as they require special care to keep in good condition. They need a large deep tank, soft acid water, a peat substrate, tall plants, and plenty of swimming space. Take live food and need some vegetable food. Eggs are laid on rocks and leaves.

River Amazon.

The Blue Discus, Green Discus and Brown Discus are all similar in shape and general variable coloring; they are sometimes considered as separate species.

75–86°F; 24–30°C 40in; 100cm

An easily kept member of the interesting cichlid family. Body greenish brown with a blue sheen on sides. Darker vertical bands on sides. Fins have greenish markings.

Easy to keep and breeds readily. Peaceable and may be kept in a community tank with larger species. Eggs are laid on rocks or substrate in the open, and eggs and young are tended by the parents, a characteristic of cichlids. Takes insects, crustaceans and worm foods.

Central America and Trinidad.

Other cichlids: the Keyhole Cichlid and the Port Acara have a distinct black blotch halfway along each side.

72–79°F; 22–26°C 24in; 60cm

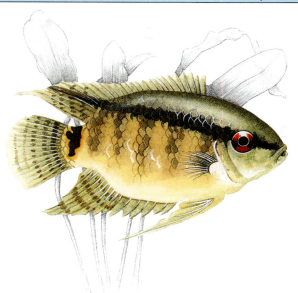

A medium-sized cichlid, with yellow to green body with several darker vertical bars. A black line runs from base of back end of dorsal fin through eye to mouth. Has a black spot bordered with yellow at the base of the tail fin.

Peaceful and rather shy, requiring a large well-planted tank with hiding places. Swims near the bottom. Quite easy to keep and breed, and can be kept in a large community tank with other large fishes, although it probably does best as a pair on their own. Lays its eggs on plants.

Guyana, River Amazon.

Firemouth Cichlid.

68–79°F; 20–26°C 24in; 60cm

FIREMOUTH CICHLID

to 6in; 15cm

The dark blue body of this cichlid contrasts sharply with the bright red belly and mouth. Large dark spot bordered with yellow on the gill cover.

Peaceful and easy to keep. Can be kept with other larger species in a community tank. Unlike some other cichlids it does not dig up all the plants in the aquarium. Takes the usual live and dried foods.

Central America: Yucatan, Guatemala.

None.

68–77°F; 20–25°C 24in; 60cm

95

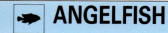

One of the most familiar of aquarium fish, with its silver and black striped disk-shaped body and wing-like dorsal and anal fins. Several color and fin varieties have been bred.

Easy to keep, but needs a tall, well-planted tank with some rocks. Swims slowly in the middle water and is best kept in a small shoal. Peaceable and suitable for a large community tank. Takes the usual live and dried foods. Eggs are laid on flat stones or surfaces of large-leaved plants.

The Amazon basin.

The slightly larger black and white Striped Fingerfish is a similar shape but fins are smaller and the tail fin has no trailing edges. It is not often seen.

72–86°F; 22–30°C 24in; 60cm

Also known as the Rio Grande Cichlid. A largish cichlid with a brown and silver patterned body and fins.

Rather aggressive and should not be kept with other species. Like some other cichlids it uproots plants and so the aquarium can be simply furnished with roots and rocks on a gravel base. Tough well-rooted plants may survive. Eggs and spawn are laid on a cleaned flat stone. Give a varied diet.

Texas and northern Mexico.

None.

75°F; 24°C 36in; 90cm

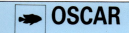

to 12in; 30cm

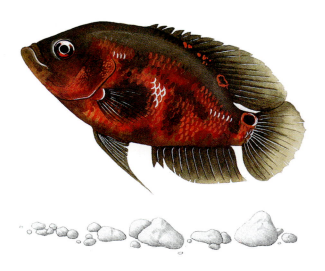

Several color forms of this large cichlid are known including the Red (illus.), Gold and Green Tiger Oscars. In the original form a greenish gray ground color is ornamented with irregular patches of dull reddish brown on sides.

Although quite easy to keep and to breed, this fish grows too large for the normal home aquarium, and is also a greedy feeder and keen digger, uprooting aquarium plants. Eggs are laid on rocks and the brood is guarded by both parents.

The Amazon, River Negro and River Paraguay.

None.

72–82°F; 22–28°C 36in; 90cm

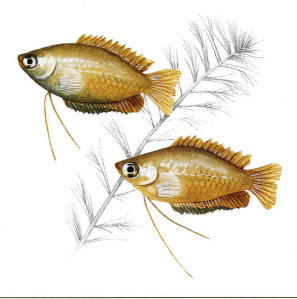

One of the smallest of the numerous gouramies now kept as aquarium fishes. It is a golden brown with a silvery sheen, the male developing a bluish-green to black throat and belly when breeding. Ventral fins modified as long thin "feelers."

Quite easy to keep and to breed, these small fish do best as a pair in their own well planted aquarium as they dislike the disturbance caused by other more active fishes. They prefer a peat substrate. They build a small nest for the eggs out of bubbles of air and saliva. Take live and dried foods.

India.

Dwarf Gourami; other gouramies are generally larger.

75–79°F; 24–26°C 16in; 40cm

Body with diagonal stripes of silver blue and bright red or reddish yellow which break up into spots on fins. Dorsal, anal and tail fin edged with red. Male more colorful, especially at breeding time.

Likes a well lit or sunny tank (to encourage algae) with dense clumps of plants and floating plants for cover. Takes live and dried food. Like most gouramies, it builds a bubble nest. A generally peaceful fish but male becomes aggressive at spawning time.

India.

Honey Gourami; other gouramies are larger.

75–81°F; 24–27°C 16in; 40cm

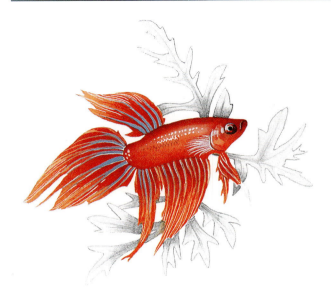

One of the best known and colorful aquarium fish, with its vividly colored rippling fins. Bright red, purple, blue and green forms have been bred. The females are less brightly colored with smaller fins.

Although males will fight viciously, tearing each other's fins to shreds, individually they are peaceable, hardy and easy to keep. A single male and one or more females may be kept in a well-planted, soft water community tank. These fish build a nest for the eggs out of bubbles of air and saliva.

Southeastern Asia.

None.

79–86°F; 26–30°C 20in; 50cm

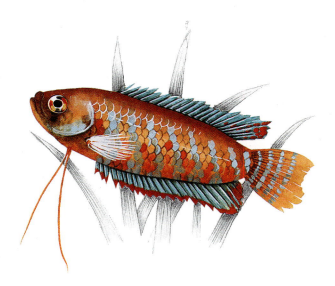

Body of male is a rich brownish red with diagonal bands of blue on side. Dorsal and anal fins mainly blue with some red. Tail red with bluish spots. Female less colorful. Ventral fins modified as long thin "feelers."

Likes a brightly lit tank to encourage algae, with dense vegetation and floating plants. A peaceful and rather shy fish which may be kept with other species, although the male becomes aggressive when ready to spawn. Takes the usual live and dried foods. Male builds a very large bubble nest.

India, Burma, Thailand and Malaysia.

The Thick-lipped Gourami is very similar in shape and coloring, with thicker lips. It is thought by some authorities to be the same species.

79°F; 26°C 16in; 40cm

A decorative fish with a pale lacy pattern ornamenting the metallic olive green body. The delicate fins also bear pale spots. A black line stretches from eye partway to tail. Throat becomes orange in male when excited.

A peaceful fish, easy to keep and which also breeds quite readily. Conditions as other gouramies, and it prefers water not too deep. Takes live and dried foods. Can be kept with other species.

Thailand, Malaysia, Borneo and Sumatra.

Moonlight Gourami: tiny scales give it a uniform silvery sheen. Three-spot Gourami: two black spots on body, the black eye making the third.

79°F; 26°C 16in; 40cm

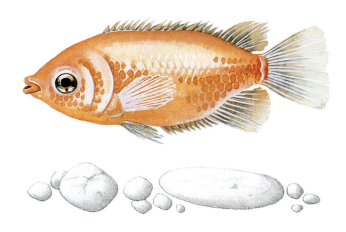

The forms usually seen in captivity have pale pinkish or yellowish bodies. There is also a dark greenish form. All have thick protruding lips. The female is noticeably stouter than the male.

A peaceful fish, suitable for a well-lit community tank when small. It is, however, largely vegetarian and greedy, and will strip soft-leaved plants rapidly. Also takes the usual dried and live foods. Takes its name from the habit of approaching and "kissing" other fish face to face.

Thailand, Malaysia, Borneo and the Indonesian islands.

Other gouramies.

68–82°F; 20–28°C 24in; 60cm

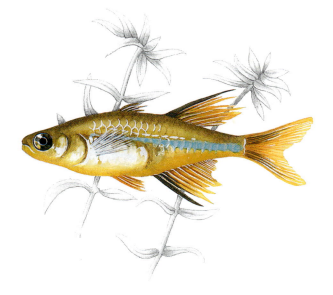

Yellow-brown body with a silvery sheen, and an extension to the anal fin and the second dorsal fin in males. The glowing blue-green line along side is most prominent towards the tail. All rainbowfishes have two dorsal fins.

A peaceful, active fish, best kept in a shoal in medium hard, slightly saline water. Takes live and dried foods. Can be kept with other species, preferably in a long tank with plenty of swimming space.

Sulawesi in the Indian Ocean.

Madagascar Rainbowfish is larger, main fins edged red and black. Dwarf Rainbowfish and Red-tailed Rainbowfish have shimmering sides and brown-edged fins.

75–81°F; 24–27°C 24in; 60cm

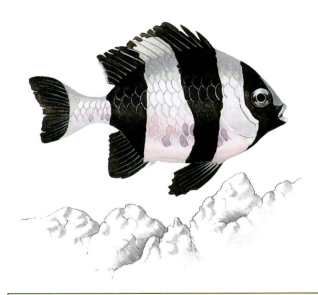

One of the black-and-white striped damselfishes, with four wide black bands including one on tail fin.

A peaceful fish, quite easy to keep in captivity. It prefers mainly live foods but can become used to taking dried food. Likes rocky cover in the tank. In the wild lives in small groups on coral reefs and rocky shores.

Seas around southeastern Asia, the Philippines, the Great Barrier Reef in Queensland and Melanesia.

The White-tailed Humbug has three black stripes and no black marking on the tail.

79–81°F; 26–27°C 40in; 100cm

106

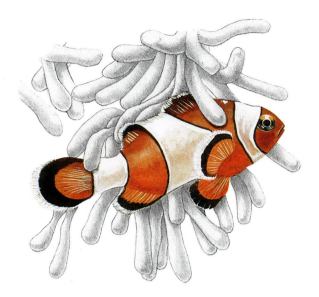

Orange body ornamented with bands of white with a distinct, black-edged white stripe behind eye. Black-edged fins add definition to the outline.

One of the more commonly kept clownfishes. In the wild clownfish always live amongst the tentacles of large sea anemones, to whose stings they are immune, but it is not necessary to provide anemones in the aquarium. One of the few tropical marine fish that has been bred in captivity.

Pacific and eastern Indian Ocean.

Similar Anemonefishes are found around Australia and Melanesia.

79–81°F; 26–27°C 32–40in; 80–100cm

The yellow-brown body has two white vertical bands, one just behind the head, the other just in front of the tail. Snout, belly and fins paler yellow.

Hardy and reported to thrive well in captivity, although not so spectacular as its relative, the Clown Anemonefish. Young fish will grow rapidly if fed frequently.

Indian Ocean from the Arabian peninsula to Indonesia.

The Spine-cheeked Anemonefish is wine red with three thin white vertical stripes, behind head, in middle of body and just before tail.

79–81°F; 26–27°C 32–40in; 80–100cm

The gorgeously colored and patterned male has a body marbled with blue, green, and orange patches divided by dark borders. There is a bright blue patch with yellow spots on gill cover. Females are drably colored.

Not an easy fish to keep. It should be kept in a species tank and fed small worms and crustaceans. It is adapted to living on the bottom.

Shallow coastal waters around Southeast Asia to Australia and Melanesia.

None.

79–81°F; 26–27°C   32–40in; 80–100cm

DUSKY ANGELFISH

to 4½in; 11.5cm

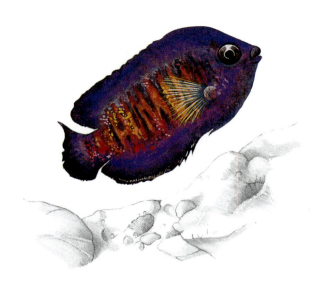

Dark purple body marked with orange and black on flanks and golden pectoral fins. A popular and hardy small angelfish.

One of the easier angelfishes to keep in captivity, as it acclimatizes and feeds readily. Likes plenty of rocky hiding places in the tank. In the wild it eats algae amongst rocks and coral.

Indian and Pacific Oceans.

None.

79–81°F; 26–27°C 32–40in; 80–100cm

LEMON PEEL

to 4in; 10cm

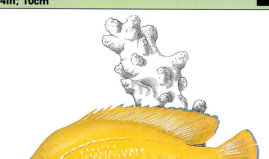

Golden yellow with tail, anal and dorsal fins edged with blue.
Young fish have a black spot in the middle of each side.

Conditions as for the Dusky Angelfish.

South Pacific.

A similar species is found around Japan.

79–81°F; 26–27°C 32–40in; 80–100cm

111

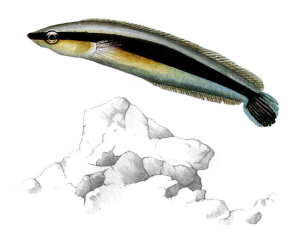

A cigar-shaped fish with a horizontal black stripe from mouth to tail, widening towards the rear. Silvery front end shades to a bluish gray at tail end.

A carnivorous, predatory fish which should be kept on its own, as it may bite chunks out of other fishes. It is easy to keep.

Around Southeast Asia and the South Pacific.

This fish mimics very closely the harmless Cleaner Wrasse and care should be taken not to confuse them.

79–81°F; 26–27°C 32in; 80cm

RED-TAILED BUTTERFLYFISH
to 6in; 15cm

Also known as the Indian Butterflyfish, it has a brown body
covered with a diagonal pattern of lighter spots. A broad white
band runs vertically behind the eye and another thinner band in
front of the eye. The tail is red.

Reported not to be too difficult to keep and feed in captivity. Like
all butterflyfishes, rather timid and requires plenty of rocky
hiding places. In the wild it feeds on algae and small crustaceans
amongst the coral. May, with patience, be persuaded to accept
dried foods in captivity.

Indian subcontinental waters to southern China.

Many other Butterflyfishes are kept in marine aquaria.
They are similarly shaped with yellow, white and orange colors
predominant.

79–81°F; 26–27°C 32–40in; 80–100cm

A distinctive fish with its brown patched body and brown spotted fins. It has poisonous dorsal spines and should be handled with extreme care.

It is carnivorous and will eat small fishes but can also be induced to take dead food. Its patterning provides excellent camouflage in its natural coral habitat as it lies in wait for prey.

Indian and Pacific Oceans.

The larger Zebra Scorpionfish or Lionfish and the related Dragonfish have brown bodies banded with numerous thin white lines and large exotically shaped fins.

79–81°F; 26–27°C 32–40in; 80–100cm

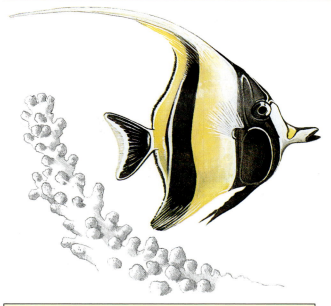

Pale yellow body with black bands and a long tapering dorsal fin. The adult develops two small "horns" close to the eyes.

A difficult fish to keep in captivity. It requires plenty of space and bright light but the color tends soon to fade.

The Indo-Pacific to the Pacific coast of Mexico. Lives in small shoals among coral.

The Pennant Butterflyfish is very similar but has a yellow tail and a narrow yellow dorsal fin continuing along the back behind the extended front edge.

79–81°F; 26–27°C 40in; 100cm

A beautiful blue fish with a clear yellow tail edged in black and a distinctive black marking on sides. Also called the Blue Tang, but see below. Surgeonfishes have two bony spikes at base of tail which can be raised as weapons.

Surgeonfishes are mainly vegetarian in the wild, feeding on algae on coral reefs, so appreciate a growth of algae in the tank. Boiled lettuce or spinach can be given instead. They can mount a fatal attack on new individuals introduced into their tank and may also attack fingers if put into the tank.

The Indian and Pacific Oceans in coral waters.

A similar Surgeonfish from the Caribbean is also known as the Blue Tang; Purple Surgeonfish: all blue with yellow tail.

81–82°F; 27–28°C 40in; 100cm

Despite their unusual outward appearance, sea-horses are fishes, with the normal internal structure of a fish. Their bodies are covered with large interlocking bony plates. This species varies in color from yellow to brown.

This delightful creature is not easy to keep in the aquarium, as it will only eat tiny live food such as brine shrimps, insect larvae or small fish. It swims upright and needs seaweed or some similar support to attach itself to by the prehensile tail to rest. Best kept in their own tank.

Indian and Pacific Oceans in coastal waters.

Several other species of sea-horse are kept in marine aquaria.

79–81°F; 26–27°C 40in; 100cm

The white body of this triggerfish is decorated with brown, blue, black and yellow in an abstract pattern, giving the fish its name.

Quite easy to keep as it readily takes small crustaceans and similar fish foods. It does, however, become aggressive when older, attacking other fishes. Triggerfishes have a spiny dorsal fin which can be "locked" upright, allowing them to wedge themselves into narrow cracks in the rock.

Indian and Pacific Oceans.

The rather similarly decorated Red Sea Picasso Fish is timid and less easy to keep.

79–81°F; 26–27°C 40in; 100cm

The large dorsal fin gives this fish a somewhat circular outline.
Brown body color is broken by stripes and spots of lighter brown.
The tail fin has a bluish tinge.

As with all surgeonfishes large amounts of vegetable food should
be given. If bought when young, this is one of the easier
surgeonfishes to keep in captivity.

The Indian and Pacific Oceans.

None.

81–82°F; 27–28°C 40in; 100cm

An elegant fish when small with a pinkish-brown body with six horizontal purple stripes, the sixth running through the dorsal fin.

A number can be kept together when small, in a tank with a sandy substrate, in which they may burrow. It can be fed on brine shrimps. In the wild it takes small crustaceans and worms from the seabed around corals.

Around East Africa, the Red Sea to southeastern Asia and the Philippines.

None.

79–81°F; 26–27°C 32–40in; 80–100cm

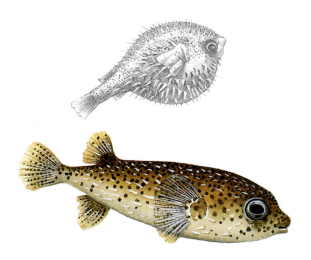

Pale yellow brown shading to a white belly, small dark dots scattered on body. Covered with sharp spines which usually lie flat on the surface, but when alarmed, the fish inflates itself to a round ball with the spines sticking out.

A good subject for the marine aquarium when young as it is easy to feed on crustaceans and small molluscs and provides a fascinating spectacle. It will, however, eventually outgrow the home aquarium.

Tropical waters in the Atlantic, Indian and Pacific Oceans.

None.

79–81°F; 26–27°C 40in; 100cm

Index and check-list

All species in Roman type are illustrated.
Keep a record by checking the boxes.

Parts of a fish

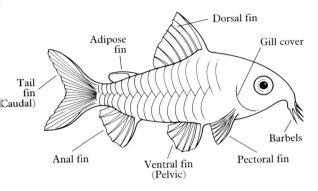

Dorsal fin

Gill cover

Adipose fin

Tail fin (Caudal)

Barbels

Anal fin

Ventral fin (Pelvic)

Pectoral fin

The Aquarium

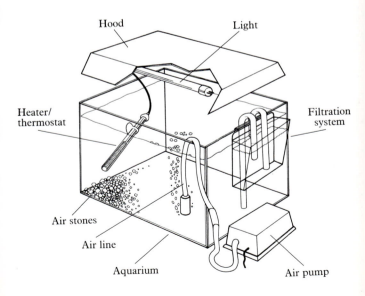

Hood

Light

Heater/ thermostat

Filtration system

Air stones

Air line

Aquarium

Air pump